Ganesha Chalisa

Published in Sanskriti Press
by Rupa Publications India Pvt. Ltd 2025
7/16, Ansari Road, Daryaganj
New Delhi 110002

Sales centres:
Bengaluru Chennai
Hyderabad Jaipur Kathmandu
Kolkata Mumbai Prayagraj

Edition copyright © Rupa Publications India Pvt. Ltd 2025

All rights reserved.
No part of this publication may be reproduced, transmitted,
or stored in a retrieval system, in any form or by any means,
electronic, mechanical, photocopying, recording or otherwise,
without the prior permission of the publisher.

P-ISBN: 978-93-5702-613-0

First impression 2025

10 9 8 7 6 5 4 3 2 1

Printed in India

This book is sold subject to the condition that it shall not, by way of
trade or otherwise, be lent, resold, hired out, or otherwise circulated,
without the publisher's prior consent, in any form of binding or cover
other than that in which it is published.

Introduction

The **Ganesha Chalisa** is a devotional hymn dedicated to Lord Ganesha, the revered Hindu god of wisdom, prosperity, remover of obstacles, and patron of arts and sciences. Written by the renowned Marathi saint **Sant Tukaram** in the 17th century, this prayer is one of the most widely recited hymns for invoking the blessings of Lord Ganesha. The term 'Chalisa' refers to a prayer composed of **forty verses**, and in the case of the Ganesha Chalisa, these verses are meant to express reverence and seek Lord Ganesha's divine intervention.

The prayer begins with an invocation to Lord Ganesha and describes his distinctive physical form, including his **elephant head**, **large belly**, and **mouse vehicle**, symbolizing humility and adaptability. As one of the most popular prayers in Hinduism, it emphasizes several key attributes of Lord Ganesha, including his power to remove obstacles (**Vighnaharta**), his association with intellect and knowledge, and his ability to bring prosperity and peace. The verses also depict his compassion and divine strength, urging devotees to call upon him for guidance and blessings in their lives.

Throughout the Chalisa, the qualities of Lord Ganesha are highlighted, such as his ability to remove obstacles and bring success, his role as the patron of intellect and wisdom, and his protective and nurturing nature. Devotees chant this prayer to invoke Ganesha's blessings not only for spiritual growth but also for material success, success in studies, and overall well-being. The prayer offers a means to seek protection from adversity and spiritual advancement in one's journey through life.

The Ganesha Chalisa holds special significance during the **Ganesh Chaturthi festival**, a time when devotees come together to celebrate the birth of Lord Ganesha. It is also commonly recited by people embarking on new ventures, journeys, or endeavors, as they seek Ganesha's intervention to ensure smooth progress and success. Reciting the Chalisa is believed to clear the mind of negativity, alleviate mental stress, and bring positivity, calm, and balance into one's life.

This hymn is typically recited with devotion and is often accompanied by the chanting of the prayer several times, with many devotees choosing to repeat it 11, 21, or 108 times. It is often sung with musical accompaniment, especially during religious festivals or private prayers. Offerings such as **modaks** (sweet dumplings that Lord Ganesha is fond of) are made while reciting the prayer as a form of devotion. The recitation helps foster a deep connection with Lord Ganesha, invoking his blessings for spiritual growth, intellectual prowess, and material success.

The Ganesha Chalisa has gained immense popularity not only in Maharashtra but across India and around the world, particularly among Indian diaspora communities. It is seen as an effective tool for overcoming life's challenges, gaining wisdom, and achieving success. For many, the prayer is a spiritual remedy, recited during moments of difficulty or when seeking clarity in life. Lord Ganesha, as a deity known for clearing paths and removing obstacles, is seen as an ideal protector and guide in times of uncertainty.

The Ganesha Chalisa, with its lyrical verses and devotional spirit, remains a powerful prayer for devotees seeking Lord Ganesha's blessings for prosperity, wisdom, and the removal of life's obstacles. Whether one is seeking guidance for intellectual pursuits, material success, or simply the grace of the divine, reciting the Ganesha Chalisa brings the devotee closer to Lord Ganesha and invites his divine presence into their life.

जय गणपति सदगुण सदन, कविवर बदन कृपाल ।
विघ्न हरण मंगल करण, जय जय गिरिजालाल ।।

Jai Ganapati Sadgun Sadan,
Kavivar Badan Kripal.
Vighna Haran Mangal Karan,
Jai Jai Girija Lal.

Victory to Lord Ganesha, the abode of all good qualities, the one with a compassionate face, who removes obstacles and is the cause of all auspiciousness. Hail, hail the son of Goddess Parvati!

1

जय जय जय गणपति गणराजू ।
मंगल भरण करण शुभ: काजू ।।

Jai Jai Jai Ganapati Ganraajoo.
Mangal Bharan Karan Shubh Kaajoo.

Hail, hail, hail Lord Ganesha, the Lord of the Ganas (divine attendants). He is the one who fills the world with auspiciousness and makes all good deeds possible.

2

जै गजबदन सदन सुखदाता ।
विश्व विनायक बुद्धि विधाता ॥

Jai Gajabdan Sadan Sukhdata.
Vishv Vinayak Buddhi Vidhata.

Hail the one with the elephant face, the giver of joy, and the remover of obstacles. He is the leader of the world, the bestower of wisdom and knowledge.

3

वक्र तुण्ड शुची शुण्ड सुहावना ।
तिलक त्रिपुण्ड भाल मन भावन ॥

Vakratund Shuchi Shund Suhavana.
Tilak Tripund Bhaal Man Bhawan.

With a curved trunk, pure and graceful, adorned with the auspicious three lines on his forehead, he captivates the mind.

4

राजत मणि मुक्तन उर माला ।
स्वर्ण मुकुट शिर नयन विशाला ।।

Rajat Mani Mukatan Ur Mala.
Swarn Mukut Shir Nayan Vishala.

He is adorned with a garland of jewels and a golden crown, his broad eyes shining like jewels.

5

पुस्तक पाणि कुठार त्रिशूलं ।
मोदक भोग सुगन्धित फूलं ॥

Pustak Pani Kuthar Trishulam.
Modak Bhog Sugandhit Phoolam.

In one hand, he holds a book, in the other a tusk and trident. He enjoys modaks (sweet offerings) and fragrant flowers.

6

सुन्दर पीताम्बर तन साजित ।
चरण पादुका मुनि मन राजित ।।

Sundar Peetambar Tan Sajeet.
Charan Paaduka Muni Man Rajit.

He is beautifully dressed in yellow robes, with his feet worshipped by the minds of sages.

7

धनि शिव सुवन षडानन भ्राता ।
गौरी लालन विश्व-विख्याता ।।

Dhanni Shiv Suvan Shadanan Bhrata.
Gauri Lalan Vishv-Vikhyata.

He is the son of Lord Shiva and the brother of Kartikeya, praised all over the world as the beloved of Goddess Gauri.

8

ऋद्धि-सिद्धि तव चंवर सुधारे ।
मुषक वाहन सोहत द्वारे ॥

Riddhi-Siddhi Tava Chamar Sudhare.
Mushak Vahan Soahat Dware.

The goddesses Riddhi and Siddhi (prosperity and success) fan him with a chime, and his mouse vehicle is poised at the door, ready to serve him.

9

कहौ जन्म शुभ कथा तुम्हारी ।
अति शुची पावन मंगलकारी ।।

Kaho Janm Shubh Katha Tumhari.
Ati Shuchi Pavan Mangalkaari.

O Lord Ganesha, tell us the story of your auspicious birth. You are pure, holy, and the source of all auspiciousness.

10

एक समय गिरिराज कुमारी ।
पुत्र हेतु तप कीन्हा भार ॥

Ek Samay Giriraj Kumari.
Putra Hetu Tap Kinha Bhari.

Once, the daughter of the mountain king, Parvati, undertook a great penance to have a son.

11

भयो यज्ञ जब पूर्ण अनूपा ।
तब पहुंच्यो तुम धरी द्विज रूपा ।।

Bhayo Yajna Jab Poorn Anupa.
Tab Pahuchyo Tum Dhari Dwij Roopa.

When the yajna (sacrifice) was complete, you appeared before her in the form of a young Brahmin boy.

12

अतिथि जानी के गौरी सुखारी ।
बहुविधि सेवा करी तुम्हारी ।।

Atithi Jani Ke Gauri Sukhari.
Bahuvidhi Seva Kari Tumhari.

Gauri (Parvati) recognized you as an honored guest and served you in many ways.

13

अति प्रसन्न हवै तुम वर दीन्हा ।
मातु पुत्र हित जो तप कीन्हा ॥

Ati Prasann Havai Tum Var Dinha.
Matu Putra Hit Jo Tap Kinha.

You were pleased and granted her the boon, fulfilling her desire for a son, a result of her penance.

14

मिलहि पुत्र तुहि, बुद्धि विशाला ।
बिना गर्भ धारण यहि काला ॥

Milhi Putra Tuhi, Buddhi Vishala.
Bina Garbh Dharan Yahi Kaala.

Ganesha, you were born to her without any physical conception, bringing intelligence and wisdom.

15

गणनायक गुण ज्ञान निधाना ।
पूजित प्रथम रूप भगवाना ॥

Gannayak Gun Gyaan Nidhana.
Poojit Pratham Roop Bhagwana.

You are the leader of the Ganas, a treasure of virtues and wisdom. You are worshipped first, before all other gods.

16

अस कही अन्तर्धान रूप हवै ।
पालना पर बालक स्वरूप हवै ॥

As Kahi Antardhaan Roop Havai.
Paalna Par Baalak Swaroop Havai.

Thus, you vanished from sight in your divine form, and appeared in the form of a child to be nurtured.

17

बनि शिशु रुदन जबहिं तुम ठाना ।
लखि मुख सुख नहिं गौरी समाना ॥

Bani Shishu Rudan Jabhim Tum Thana.
Lakhi Mukh Sukh Nahin Gauri Samana.

When you began to cry as a baby, Goddess Parvati (Gauri) could not bear the sight of it, feeling immense joy and sorrow at the same time.

18

सकल मगन, सुखमंगल गावहिं ।
नाभ ते सुरन, सुमन वर्षावहिं ॥

Sakal Magan, Sukhmangal Gaavahin.
Naabh Te Suran, Suman Varshaavhin.

When you appeared, all gods and sages sang songs of joy, and flowers rained down from the skies in celebration.

19

शम्भु, उमा, बहुदान लुटावहिं ।
सुर मुनिजन, सुत देखन आवहिं ॥

Shambhu, Uma, Bahudan Lutaavhin.
Sur Munijan, Sut Dekhan Aavhin.

Lord Shiva, Goddess Uma, and many other divine beings showered their blessings upon you, and all the gods and sages came to see you.

20

लखि अति आनन्द मंगल साजा ।
देखन भी आये शनि राजा ॥

Lakhi Ati Anand Mangal Saja.
Dekhan Bhi Aaye Shani Raja.

Lord Ganesha's arrival brought immense joy and auspiciousness, and even Lord Shani (the planet Saturn) came to witness this divine moment.

21

निज अवगुण गुनि शनि मन माहीं ।
बालक, देखन चाहत नाहीं ॥

Nij avagun guni shani man maahi.
Baalak, dekhan chaahat naahi.

Lord Shani reflects on his own faults and imperfections, yet the child (Lord Ganesha) does not wish to be concerned with such flaws.

22

गिरिजा कछु मन भेद बढायो ।
उत्सव मोर, न शनि तुही भायो ॥

Girija kachu man bhed badhayo.
Utsav mor, na shani tuhi bhaayo.

Goddess Parvati felt some inner conflict, but the joyous celebration of Lord Ganesha's arrival was so powerful that even Lord Shani was not affected by fear or negativity.

23

कहत लगे शनि, मन सकुचाई ।
का करिहौ, शिशु मोहि दिखाई ।।

Kahat lage shani, man sakuchai. Kaa kariho, shishu mohi dikhai.

Lord Shani hesitated and spoke softly, wondering what he could do when he saw the innocent child (Lord Ganesha).

24

नहिं विश्वास, उमा उर भयऊ ।
शनि सों बालक देखन कहयऊ ॥

Nahīn vishwas, Uma ur bhayu. Shani son baalak dekhan kahayoo.

Goddess Parvati was filled with doubt and fear in her heart, expressing concern about Lord Shani's gaze upon the child.

25

पदतहिं शनि दृग कोण प्रकाशा ।
बालक सिर उड़ि गयो अकाशा ॥

Padahin shani drig kon prakasha.
Baalak sir uḍi gayo akasha.

Lord Shani's powerful gaze illuminated the atmosphere, and Lord Ganesha's head flew off, soaring into the sky.

26

गिरिजा गिरी विकल हवै धरणी ।
सो दुःख दशा गयो नहीं वरणी ॥

Girija giri vikala havai dharani.
So dukh dasha gayo nahin varani.

Goddess Parvati was deeply distressed, and the earth trembled. The situation was so painful that it could not even be described.

27

हाहाकार मच्यौ कैलाशा ।
शनि कीन्हों लखि सुत को नाशा ॥

Hahakaar machayo Kailasha.
Shani keenho lakhii sut ko naasha.

A great uproar echoed through Mount Kailash, as Lord Shani realized his mistake and caused the destruction of the child's head.

28

तुरत गरुड़ चढ़ि विष्णु सिधायो ।
काटी चक्र सो गज सिर लाये ॥

Turat Garud chadh Vishnu sidhayo.
Kaati chakra so gaj sir laaye.

Lord Vishnu mounted Garuda and swiftly used his Sudarshan Chakra to bring back an elephant's head for Lord Ganesha.

29

बालक के धड़ ऊपर धारयो ।
प्राण मन्त्र पढ़ि शंकर डारयो ।।

Baalak ke dhad upar dhaaryo.
Praan mantra padh Shankar daaryo.

The elephant's head was placed on Lord Ganesha's body, and Lord Shiva recited a life-giving mantra to restore his life.

30

नाम गणेश शम्भु तब कीन्हे ।
प्रथम पूज्य बुद्धि निधि, वर दीन्हे ॥

Naam Ganesha Shambhu tab keenhe.
Pratham poojya buddhi nidhi, var deenhē.

Lord Shiva named the child Ganesha and granted him the boon of being the first to be worshiped and the keeper of wisdom.

31

बुद्धि परीक्षा जब शिव कीन्हा ।
पृथ्वी कर प्रदक्षिणा लीन्हा ॥

Buddhi pariksha jab Shiv keenha.
Prithvi kar pradakshina leenha.

Lord Shiva tested Lord Ganesha's wisdom, and Ganesha circumambulated the Earth as part of the test.

32

चले षडानन, भरमि भुलाई ।
रचे बैठ तुम बुद्धि उपाई ॥

Chale Shadanan, bharami bhulai.
Rache baith tum buddhi upai.

Lord Kartikeya, Lord Shiva's son, got confused and left on his journey, while Lord Ganesha sat down and devised a clever solution.

33

चरण मातु-पितु के धर लीन्हें ।
तिनके सात प्रदक्षिण कीन्हें ॥

*Charan maatu-pitu ke dhar leenhe.
Tinke saath pradakshina keenhe.*

Lord Ganesha placed his feet on his parents' feet and circumambulated them seven times as a gesture of devotion.

34

धनि गणेश कही शिव हिये हरषे ।
नभ ते सुरन सुमन बहु बरसे ॥

Dhanni Ganesha kahi Shiv hiye harashe.
Nabh te suran suman bahu barse.

Lord Shiva, with great joy in his heart, praised Ganesha, and flowers rained down from the heavens in celebration.

35

तुम्हरी महिमा बुद्धि बड़ाई ।
शेष सहसमुख सके न गाई ॥

Tumhari mahima buddhi barai. Shesh sahasamukh sake na gai.

The glory and greatness of Lord Ganesha's wisdom were so vast that even Sheshnag, with his many mouths, could not fully sing his praises.

36

मैं मतिहीन मलीन दुखारी ।
करहूं कौन विधि विनय तुम्हारी ।।

Main matiheen maleen dukhaari.
Karhoon kaun vidhi vinay tumhaari.

I, being ignorant and troubled, am unable to express the greatness of Ganesha, and with my limited wisdom, I wonder how I can properly offer my reverence.

37

भजत रामसुन्दर प्रभुदासा ।
जग प्रयाग, ककरा, दुर्वासा ॥

Bhajat Ramsundar prabhudasa.
Jag prayag, kakra, durvasa.

I am a humble servant of Lord Ram, and I praise His name, which purifies the world, just like the sacred confluence of Prayag.

38

अब प्रभु दया दीना पर कीजै ।
अपनी शक्ति भक्ति कुछ दीजै ।।

Ab prabhu daya deena par kijai.
Apni shakti bhakti kuch dijai.

Now, Lord, I seek your mercy and grace, and I ask for your strength and devotion.

39

हर कार्य में तुम हो,
विघ्न विनाशक गणपति ।
सिद्धि और रिद्धि के साथ,
धन लक्ष्मी है तू गणपति ॥

Har Karya Mein Tum Ho,
Vighna Vinashak Ganapati.
Siddhi Aur Riddhi Ke Saath,
Dhan Lakshmi Hai Tu Ganapati.

Lord Ganesha, you are present in all works and remove every obstacle. Along with the goddesses Siddhi and Riddhi, you bestow wealth and prosperity.

40

विष्णु जी की मूर्ति,
शंकर भगवान की पूजित ।
सकल सुख देने वाला,
श्री गणेश जी की पूजा ही पूजित ॥

Vishnu Ji Ki Murti,
Shankar Bhagwan Ki Poojit.
Sakal Sukh Dene Wala,
Shree Ganesh Ji Ki Pooja Hi Poojit.

Lord Ganesha is revered like Lord Vishnu and Lord Shiva. He is the bestower of all happiness and success, and his worship brings the highest blessings.

श्री गणेश यह चालीसा, पाठ करै कर ध्यान ।
नित नव मंगल गृह बसै, लहे जगत सन्मान ॥

Shri Ganesh Yah Chalisa, Paath Karai Kar Dhyaan.
Nit Nav Mangal Grih Basai, Lahe Jagat Sanmaan.

सम्बन्ध अपने सहस्त्र दश, ऋषि पंचमी दिनेश ।
पूरण चालीसा भयो, मंगल मूर्ती गणेश ॥

Sambandh Apne Sahastra Dash, Rishi Panchami Dinesh.
Puran Chaleesa Bhayo, Mangal Moorti Ganesh.

गणेश आरती

जय गणेश जय गणेश, जय गणेश देवा ।
माता जाकी पार्वती, पिता महादेवा ॥

एक दंत दयावंत, चार भुजा धारी ।
माथे सिंदूर सोहे, मूसे की सवारी ॥

जय गणेश जय गणेश, जय गणेश देवा ।
माता जाकी पार्वती, पिता महादेवा ॥

पान चढ़े फल चढ़े, और चढ़े मेवा ।
लड्डूअन का भोग लगे, संत करें सेवा ॥

जय गणेश जय गणेश, जय गणेश देवा ।
माता जाकी पार्वती, पिता महादेवा ॥

अंधन को आंख देत, कोढ़िन को काया ।
बांझन को पुत्र देत, निर्धन को माया ।।

जय गणेश जय गणेश, जय गणेश देवा ।
माता जाकी पार्वती, पिता महादेवा ।।

श्सूरश् श्याम शरण आए, सफल कीजे सेवा ।
माता जाकी पार्वती, पिता महादेवा ।।

जय गणेश जय गणेश, जय गणेश देवा ।
माता जाकी पार्वती, पिता महादेवा ।।

दीनन की लाज रखो, शंभु सुतकारी ।
कामना को पूर्ण करो, जाऊं बलिहारी ।।

जय गणेश जय गणेश, जय गणेश देवा ।
माता जाकी पार्वती, पिता महादेवा ।।

Ganesh Aarti

Jai Ganesh Jai Ganesh, Jai Ganesh Deva.
Mata Jaaki Parvati, Pita Mahadeva.

Ek Dant Dayavant, Char Bhujha Dhaari.
Mathe Sindoor Sohe, Moose Ki Sawari.

Jai Ganesh Jai Ganesh, Jai Ganesh Deva.
Mata Jaaki Parvati, Pita Mahadeva.

Paan Chhade Phal Chhade, Aur Chhade Meva.
Ladduan Ka Bhog Lage, Sant Kare Seva.

Jai Ganesh Jai Ganesh, Jai Ganesh Deva.
Mata Jaaki Parvati, Pita Mahadeva.

Andhan Ko Aankh Det, Kodin Ko Kaaya.
Baanjan Ko Putra Det, Nirdhan Ko Maya.

Jai Ganesh Jai Ganesh, Jai Ganesh Deva.
Mata Jaaki Parvati, Pita Mahadeva.

'Sur' Shyam Sharan Aaye, Safal Kije Seva.
Mata Jaaki Parvati, Pita Mahadeva.

Jai Ganesh Jai Ganesh, Jai Ganesh Deva.
Mata Jaaki Parvati, Pita Mahadeva.

Deenan Ki Laaj Rakho, Shambhu Sutkaari.
Kamna Ko Poorn Karo, Jaaoon Balihari.

Jai Ganesh Jai Ganesh, Jai Ganesh Deva.
Mata Jaaki Parvati, Pita Mahadeva.